I0018459

Printing
Easy Excel Essentials
Volume 6

M.L. HUMPHREY

Copyright © 2017-2018 M.L. Humphrey

All rights reserved.

ISBN: 978-1-950902-35-4

Also published under ISBN 978-1720564416

TITLES BY M.L. HUMPHREY

EASY EXCEL ESSENTIALS
Pivot Tables
Conditional Formatting
Charts
The IF Functions
Formatting
Printing

EXCEL ESSENTIALS
Excel for Beginners
Intermediate Excel
50 Useful Excel Functions
50 More Excel Functions

EXCEL ESSENTIALS QUIZ BOOKS
The Excel for Beginners Quiz Book
The Intermediate Excel Quiz Book
The 50 Useful Excel Functions Quiz Book
The 50 More Excel Functions Quiz Book

DATA PRINCIPLES
Data Principles for Beginners

BUDGETING FOR BEGINNERS
Budgeting for Beginners
Excel for Budgeting

WORD ESSENTIALS
Word for Beginners
Intermediate Word

MAIL MERGE
Mail Merge for Beginners

POWERPOINT ESSENTIALS
PowerPoint for Beginners

.

CONTENTS

Introduction   1

Printing   3

Conclusion   15

Appendix: Basic Terminology   17

INTRODUCTION

In *Excel for Beginners* I covered the basics of working in Excel, including how to format in Excel and how to print. In *Intermediate Excel* I covered a number of intermediate-level topics such as pivot tables, charts, and conditional formatting. And in *50 Useful Excel Functions* I covered fifty of the most useful functions you can use in Excel.

But I realize that some users will just want to know about a specific topic and not buy a guide that covers a variety of other topics that aren't of interest to them.

So this series of guides is meant to address that need. Each guide in the series covers one specific topic such as pivot tables, conditional formatting, or charts.

I'm going to assume in these guides that you have a basic understanding of how to navigate Excel, although each guide does include an Appendix with a brief discussion of basic terminology to make sure that we're on the same page.

The guides are written using Excel 2013, which should be similar enough for most users of Excel to follow, but anyone using a version of Excel prior to Excel 2007 probably won't be able to use them effectively.

Also, keep in mind that the content in these guides is drawn from *Excel for Beginners, Intermediate Excel,* and/or *50 Useful Excel Functions,* so if you think you'll end up buying more than one or two of these guides you're probably better off just buying *Excel for Beginners, Intermediate Excel,* and/or *50 Useful Excel Functions.*

With that said, let's talk about how to print documents from Excel.

PRINTING

Learning how to print documents from Excel, and how to format documents that you create so that they print nicely, is essential. I can't count the number of times someone has sent me a document, I've clicked on print without thinking, and ended up with page after page of fractured garbage. Tables split across pages, no header rows to tell me what I'm looking at, no column on the left-hand side that repeats to tie together different entries, etc.

Don't be that person that sends someone a file that prints horribly. (Although we've all been that person at some point in time.)

First things first.

To print you can either use Ctrl + P or go to the File tab and select Print from there.

If you don't want to clean anything up, you can then just click on the big Print button at the top of the page and be done with it, but I highly highly recommend that you at least look through the Print Preview to see if the document looks like you think it should.

In current versions of Excel the Print Preview appears by default on the right-hand side of the screen and you can page through it using the arrows at the bottom and to the left of the preview. In older versions of Excel you'll have to choose to look at the Print Preview.

The rest of this initial discussion is going to use the Print screen as seen in Excel 2013. For those of you with pre-2007 versions of Excel you'll have to make your adjustments using the Print dialogue box, but the discussion of what each of these options mean will still be useful to you.

So here is the list of print options you should see when you use Ctrl + P or go to the Print section of the File tab.

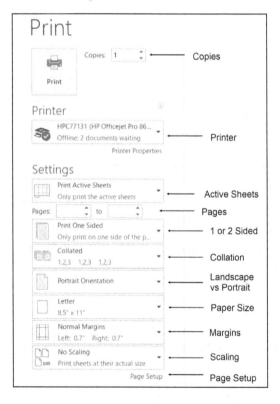

We're going to walk through each of them, starting at the top and working our way down.

Print

Once you're ready to print your page, you can click on the button on the top left with the image of a printer that says Print under it. This will print your document.

Number of Copies

The number of copies to print is displayed to the right of the printer icon. If you want to print more than one copy, change this number to the number of copies you want. You can either use the up and down arrows next to the Print button until you reach the desired number of copies, or click into the box and type the number of copies you want.

Printer

Directly below the print icon is where you select the printer you want to use. It should display your computer's default printer. Sometimes it will instead display the most recently used printer.

If you want to use a different printer than the one shown, click on the arrow next to the printer name and choose from the listed options.

If the printer you want isn't listed, choose Add Printer and add the printer.

Print Active Sheets /
Print Entire Workbook / Print Selection

The next option after that is what you want to print.

My version of Excel defaults to Print Active Sheets. This will generally be the worksheet you were working in when you chose to print. However, it is possible to select more than one worksheet by holding down the Control key while you click on each worksheet name. When you do this, you'll see that the names of all of your selected worksheets are now highlighted. In Excel 2013 that means they are colored white instead of gray and the name is bolded. The one you're currently on will have green text and the other selected worksheets will have black.

If you've done this, then when you choose to Print Active Sheets all of the selected sheets will print, not just the one you were on when you chose to print.

I would only print multiple worksheets if you're satisfied that each one is formatted the way you want it formatted.

Also, choosing to print more than one sheet at a time, either with Print Active Sheets or Print Entire Workbook, will result in your headers and footers being combined as if it's all one document. If you mean each worksheet to be a standalone report with numbered pages specific to that report, then you need to print each worksheet separately.

As I just alluded to, the Print Entire Workbook option prints all of the worksheets in your workbook.

Print Selection allows you to just print a highlighted section of a worksheet or worksheets. This can be very useful if you just want a few rows from an existing worksheet, but be careful if you combine it with selecting multiple worksheets, because it will print that range of selected cells from each of the selected worksheets.

(I happened to have three worksheets selected at once and when I highlighted the first twenty cells in one of those worksheets, the selection it was ready to print was those twenty cells in each of the three worksheets.)

Print Selected Pages

Directly below that option is where you can choose to print selected pages within the selection. It says Pages and has two boxes with arrows at the side that are blank by default.

You can use this option to just print a specific page or pages from those that are shown in the print preview. So if the preview shows four pages, but page 4 in the preview is the only one you want then you'd enter 4 into both boxes and when you click on Print Excel will only print that fourth page that was shown in the preview.

Print One Sided /
Print on Both Sides (long edge) /
Print on Both Sides (short edge)

By default Excel will print your document on one side of the page.

If you have a printer that can print on both sides of the page you can change this setting to do that.

Use the long-edge option if your layout is going to be portrait-style and the short-edge option if your layout is going to be landscape-style.

Collated / Uncollated

You only need to worry about collation if you're printing more than one copy of a multi-page document.

In that case, you need to decide if you want to print one full copy at a time, x number of times (collated) or if you want to print x copies of page 1 and then x copies of page 2 and then x copies of page 3 and so on until you've printed all pages of your document (uncollated).

Usually you'll want collated which is also the default.

Portrait Orientation /
Landscape Orientation

You can choose to print in either portrait orientation (with the short edge of the page on top, which is standard for most books and reports) or landscape orientation (with the long edge of the page on top, which you often see with, for example, PowerPoint presentations).

You can see the difference by changing the option in Excel and looking at your print preview.

For me which option I choose depends mostly on how many columns of data I have. Assuming I'm dealing with a normal worksheet with rows of data listed across various columns, my goal is to fit all of my columns on one page if possible. And sometimes changing the layout to landscape allows me to do that, because it allows me to have more columns per page than I'd be able to fit in portrait mode.

If I have just a few columns of data, but lots of rows I'll generally stick with portrait orientation instead.

You'll have to decide what works best for you.

Letter / Legal / Statement / Etc.

This is where you select your paper type. It defaults to Letter, so 8.5"x11" here in the U.S. and probably A4 overseas. If you need to print on legal paper or some other size, this is where you'd make that choice.

This may sound obvious, but just in case, be sure that the printer you're printing to actually has the paper size you choose. For example, I'm sure my printer could print on legal paper but I don't have any available to use so there's no point in my selecting that paper size. (Also, if you're setting up a document for someone else to print, try to stick to standard paper sizes that they're likely to have.)

Normal Margins / Wide Margins / Narrow Margins / Custom Margins

I would expect you won't use this, but this is where you can change the margins on a document.

The normal margins in Excel 2013 for the U.S. allow for .7" on each side and .75" on top and bottom. The wide margin option has 1" all the way around and the narrow margin option has .75" top and bottom and .25" on the sides.

If you have a lot of text and need just a little more room to fit it all on one page, you could use the narrow margin option to make that happen.

(I generally use the scaling option instead.)

No Scaling / Fit Sheet on One Page / Fit All Columns on One Page / Fit All Rows on One Page

Scaling is something I use often.

Each time I run into a situation where my columns are just a little bit too wide to fit on the page or I have just a few too many rows to fit on the page, I fix it with scaling.

If you choose "Fit All Columns on One Page" that will make sure that all of your columns fit across the top of one page. You might still have multiple pages because of the number of rows, but at least everything will fit across one page.

Fit All Rows on One Page is good for if you have maybe one or two rows too many to naturally fit on the page.

Fit Sheet on One Page is a combination of fitting all columns and all rows onto one page.

Be careful with all of these options, though. Because Excel will do exactly what you tell it to do. If you have fifty columns and tell Excel to fit all columns on one page it will do so. Unfortunately, it'll do so by shrinking the font size to such a small size you won't be able to read it.

So always be sure to look at your print preview before you print when using scaling.

I often find it helps to combine a landscape print orientation with fit all columns on one page. If, however, what you really need is a document that's 2 pages across by 5 pages long then you need to use the Page Setup scaling option instead.

Page Setup

The Page Setup link at the very bottom of the list of options gives you access to the Page Setup dialogue box which allows you to do even more.

As with everything else in the more modern versions of Excel, the most obvious options are the ones that are readily visible that we already discussed, but those aren't the only options.

If you click on the Page Setup link you'll be taken to the Page Setup dialogue box which gives you another way to choose your print options. (And is the old way of doing things for those of you in older versions of Excel.)

A few things to point out to you that I find useful:

Scaling

On the Page tab you can see the scaling option once more. But the nice thing here is that you can specify any number of pages across and any number of pages long. You're not limited to 1 page wide or 1 page tall.

So say you have a document that's currently one page wide and four pages long but that fourth page contains just one row. You can scale that document in the Page Setup dialogue box so that the document that prints is one page wide by three pages long and that last row is brought up onto the prior page.

Center Horizontally or Vertically

On the Margins tabs there are two check boxes that let you center what you're printing either horizontally or vertically or both.

I often choose to center items vertically so that they're centered on the page. Otherwise they look off balance.

Header/Footer

We're going to talk about another way to do this in a moment, but if you want to set up a header and/or a footer for your printed document you can do so here. The dropdown boxes that say (none) include a number of pre-formatted headers and footers for you to use.

So if you just want the page number included, for example, there are pre-formatted headers and footers that allow you to do so.

Same with including the worksheet name or file name in the header or footer.

As you look at each one it will show you examples of the actual text that will be included.

You also have the option of customizing either the header or footer, although that can be more tricky to do.

Sheet

The sheet tab has a couple of useful options, but I'm going to show you a different way to set these options because I find it easier to use them when I'm in the worksheet itself.

* * *

Page Layout Tab

If you exit out of the print option and go back to your worksheet, you'll see that one of the tabs you have available to use is called Page Layout. There are certain attributes that I set up here before I print my documents. (Or, more often, come back to after I start working in the print setup.)

You'll also note that you can change your document margins, orientation, and size here as well.

Print Area

If you only want to print a portion of a worksheet, you can set that portion as your print area by highlighting it and then clicking on the arrow next to Print Area and choosing Set Print Area.

Only do it this way (as opposed to highlighting the section and choosing Print-Selection) if it's a permanent setting. This is because once you set your print area it will remain set until you clear it and it's easy to forget you've done so, add more data to your worksheet, and then not know that the new data wasn't included when you printed the document.

So I use this when I have a worksheet that has either a lot of extra information I'll never want to print or where the formatting extends beyond my data and Excel keeps trying to print all those empty but formatted cells.

Breaks

You can specify where page breaks occur in your worksheet using the Breaks dropdown.

So say you have a worksheet that takes up four pages and you want to make sure that rows 1 through 10 are on a page together and then rows 11 through 20 are on a page together even though that's not how things would naturally fall. You can set a page break to force that to happen.

(Personally, I find page breaks a challenge to work with, so I usually try to get what I need some other way.)

Print Titles

This one is incredibly valuable. What it lets you do is set a row or rows and a column or columns that will repeat on every single page.

So, for example, let's say you have a table of data that when printed is two pages wide and ten pages long. How do you know on that second page which entries you're looking at? Or on that tenth page what all the columns of data are. If you have data where that's not obvious, using Print Titles lets you set up your document so that the header row(s) and the identifier column(s) repeat on every single page.

When you click on Print Titles, you'll see that it brings up the Page Setup dialogue box and takes you to the Sheet tab.

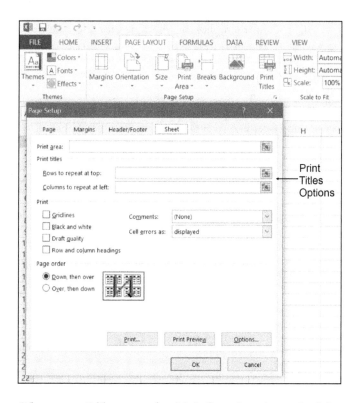

(The reason I like to work with it from here instead of the Print screen is because I can easily just click in the box I need and then go directly to my worksheet to select my rows or columns I need to repeat. If I were to use this from the Print screen I'd have to know the rows and columns I wanted to use and how to write them in cell notation.)

"Rows to repeat at top" is where you specify what row(s) is your header row. Click in that box and then click on the row number in your worksheet that you want to have repeat at the top of each page. Excel will convert that into cell notation for you.

"Columns to repeat at left" is where you specify what column(s) you need to repeat on each of your pages. Click in that box and then click on the letter for the column(s) you want to repeat on each page. Excel will convert that into cell notation for you as well.

Be careful if you're going to choose more than one row or column to repeat that you don't end up selecting so many rows or columns that you basically just print the same thing over and over and over again. (It's happened.)

CONCLUSION

So that's it for printing. Lots of options available to you. I would say that orientation, scaling, print titles and printing two-sided are probably the ones I find the most useful. Then again, these days I don't do a lot of work presentations. When that was the case collation, being able to select a printer, and changing my paper size were just as important to me.

The key, whatever you use, is that you want anything you print from Excel to be easy to read and understand and to not waste a bunch of paper unnecessarily.

If you get stuck, reach out. I'm happy to help. I don't check that email account every single day but I do check it regularly and will try to find you the answer if I don't know it.

Good luck with it!

APPENDIX A: BASIC TERMINOLOGY

Column

Excel uses columns and rows to display information. Columns run across the top of the worksheet and, unless you've done something funky with your settings, are identified using letters of the alphabet.

Row

Rows run down the side of the worksheet and are numbered starting at 1 and up to a very high number.

Cell

A cell is a combination of a column and row that is identified by the letter of the column it's in and the number of the row it's in. For example, Cell A1 is the cell in the first column and first row of a worksheet.

Click

If I tell you to click on something, that means to use your mouse (or trackpad) to move the arrow on the screen over to a specific location and left-click or right-click on the option. (See the next definition for the difference between left-click and right-click).

If you left-click, this selects the item. If you right-click, this generally creates a dropdown list of options to choose from. If I don't tell you which to do, left- or right-click, then left-click.

Left-click/Right-click

If you look at your mouse or your trackpad, you generally have two flat buttons to press. One is on the left side, one is on the right. If I say left-click that means to press down on the button on the left. If I say right-click that means press down on the button on the right. (If you're used to using Word or Excel you may already do this without even thinking about it. So, if that's the case then think of left-click as what you usually use to select text and right-click as what you use to see a menu of choices.)

Spreadsheet

I'll try to avoid using this term, but if I do use it, I'll mean your entire Excel file. It's a little confusing because it can sometimes also be used to mean a specific worksheet, which is why I'll try to avoid it as much as possible.

Worksheet

This is the term I'll use as much as possible. A worksheet is a combination of rows and columns that you can enter data in. When you open an Excel file, it opens to worksheet one.

Formula Bar

This is the long white bar at the top of the screen with the $f\chi$ symbol next to it.

Tab

I refer to the menu choices at the top of the screen (File, Home, Insert, Page Layout, Formulas, Data, Review, and View) as tabs. Note how they look like folder tabs from an old-time filing system when selected? That's why.

Data

I use data and information interchangeably. Whatever information you put into a worksheet is your data.

Select

If I tell you to "select" cells, that means to highlight them.

Arrow

If I say that you can "arrow" to something that just means to use the arrow keys to navigate from one cell to another.

A1:A25

If I'm going to reference a range of cells, I'll use the shorthand notation that Excel uses in its formulas. So, for example, A1:A25 will mean Cells A1 through A25. If you ever don't understand exactly what I'm referring to, you can type it into a cell in Excel using the = sign and see what cells Excel highlights. So, =A1:A25 should highlight cells A1 through A25 and =A1:B25 should highlight the cells in columns A and B and rows 1 through 25.

With Formulas Visible

Normally Excel doesn't show you the formula in a cell unless you click on that cell and then you only see the formula in the formula bar. But to help you see what I'm referring to, some of the screenshots in this guide will be provided with formulas visible. All this means is that I clicked on Show Formulas on the Formulas tab so that you could see what cells have formulas in them and what those formulas are.

Unless you do the same, your worksheet will not look like that. That's okay. Because you don't need to have your formulas visible unless you're troubleshooting something that isn't working.

Dialogue Box

I will sometimes reference a dialogue box. These are the boxes that occasionally pop up with additional options for you to choose from for that particular task. Usually I include a screen shot so you know what it should look like.

Paste Special – Values

I will sometimes suggest that you paste special-values. What this means is to paste your data using the Values option under Paste Options (the one with 123 on the clipboard). This will paste the values from the cells you copied without also bringing over any of the formulas that created those values.

Dropdown

I will occasionally refer to a dropdown or dropdown menu. This is generally a list of potential choices that you can select from. The existence of the list is indicated by an arrow next to the first available selection. I will occasionally refer to the list of options you see when you click on a dropdown arrow as the dropdown menu.

ABOUT THE AUTHOR

M.L. Humphrey is a former stockbroker with a degree in Economics from Stanford and an MBA from Wharton who has spent close to twenty years as a regulator and consultant in the financial services industry.

You can reach M.L. at mlhumphreywriter@gmail.com or at mlhumphrey.com.